Papier Mâché

*Peter Rush is an illustrator of
children's books. Having trained as an
artist at St Martin's School of Art in
London, he spent three working years
in America. Since his return he has
become well known through his
contributions to the illustrations used
on the BBC television programme*
Jackanory *over the past twelve years.
He took to papier mâché originally as
a relief from so much drawing, and
several of his models have been
photographed for the* Sunday
Telegraph Magazine. *He now lives
in Scotland with his wife and three
children.*

Peter Rush

Papier Mâché

Canongate

First published in 1980
by Canongate Publishing Ltd,
17 Jeffrey Street, Edinburgh
© Peter Rush 1980
Colour photographs © Victor Albrow 1980
ISBN 0 903937 89 1
Printed in Great Britain by
Butler & Tanner Ltd, Frome, Somerset

**Colour photographs by Victor Albrow.
Photographs on pages 1 and 85 by
Pat Keene; photograph on page 93 by
Irene Barry.
All drawings by the author.**

Contents

Trees are poems written against the sky, which we fell to write our own emptiness on.

Kahil Gibran

Introduction

About fourteen years ago, a young designer came to see me at the magazine offices. Unlike most, he wasn't accompanied by the usual large black portfolio, but carried an immaculate custom-built case.

It was opened to reveal a set of the most perfect papier mâché figures that I had seen, for they went far beyond my preconceived ideas of this particular art form. This was my introduction to Peter Rush's work.

Over the years Peter has provided a marvellous range of models. Commissions have ranged from a full-size Jersey cow to a series of portrait characters of famous people in prehistoric guise!

This delightful book tells us how it can be achieved. The only thing missing is the one secret ingredient, the touch of magic that only Peter Rush possesses.

Geof Axby
art director *Sunday Telegraph Magazine*

for Jane and for Stephanie

I would like to thank Suzi Siddons for her generous help and vigorous editing

# *Foreword*

I would like to explain how the approach here to modelling in paper differs from that in other books on the subject.

Firstly, since 1900 the most outstanding influence on the development of papier mâché has been the consistent use of newspaper as its basic material and this has really determined what can be attempted.

Newspaper is considered here as only one of the long list of possible papers and materials open to us. Each kind of paper is seen to have its own characteristics and is usually good for modelling just one or two things. So, if we are cunning, we choose exactly the right paper to achieve our end with the minimum of fuss. All we need to know of any paper is: what kind of folds and creases will it make?

Medium-thick brown paper, for example, simulates canvas or raincoat material. Thick brown paper for leather. Tissue paper is excellent for lace and cotton: pulled taut it imitates satin. Typing paper is ideal for shirts and heavy skirts: doubled up it works well for suits and military clothing. Paper handkerchiefs are very good for picking up the characteristics of loose skin and so on. Newspaper, in fact, being very stiff and springy, is rarely used.

Introduced to papier mâché as a schoolchild, the initial spark of interest was dampened down for twenty years under this soggy grey newspaper mash, and I'm afraid that lumpy looking ashtrays and nut bowls did little to revive it. Perhaps I was unlucky; nevertheless, it still happens to children today.

When we use tissue paper softened with cellulose wall-paper paste, we are using the very same organic materials that we are trying to simulate, ie tissue and cells. In the making of a head, for example, the tissue paper is packed hard and tight for bone (forehead, cheekbones and bridge of the nose); made into small rolls and pulled taut we have the muscles. Small pieces of tissue paper laid over these muscles become skin, and pulled out into fine fibrous shreds we have hair. The effect of all this can be startlingly realistic.

When the model is completed and dry before painting, it is given a coat of white emulsion. This not only conveniently fills up the cracks and helps to unite the model, but all the different types of paper and materials that have been used become neutralized under this fresh white skin. Part of the interest is then that anyone looking at the model is at a loss to know either how it was made or from what material.

The development of
papier mâché

By the end of the second century AD the Chinese had invented paper, made then from mulberry bark, cotton, vegetable fibre and linen rags. Paper making was slow, laborious work and therefore expensive, so it would follow that good use was put to off-cuts and scrap. Two papier mâché helmets, toughened by being lacquered, survive from this period and these are the first examples of papier mâché that we know of. It is interesting to us, who, over the last fifty years or so, have come to think of papier mâché as an essentially transitory medium, that it should have ever been used for something so serious as armour, and also that a specimen should survive for nearly two thousand years.

From China, paper making spread to Japan and to Persia where it was used largely for making masks and festival ornaments. By AD 900 the technique of moulding paper, stiffened and waterproofed with copal varnish, was known in Europe, and by the seventeenth century this technique was being used extensively for small, useful and decorative

11

objects; papier mâché manufacture grew rapidly in confidence and dexterity through the eighteenth and nineteenth centuries, culminating in the ornate and elaborately decorated furnishings that we see in museums.

Towards the end of the seventeenth century we know of a manufacturer called Wilton of Charing Cross, London, who was producing architectural mouldings, cornices, scrolls, rosettes, wall brackets and decorative ornaments for attaching to chimney pieces, and furniture made from papier mâché; these weighing only a fraction of their plaster and stucco counterparts. It was through her trade with the Orient that England was attracted to the decorative side of papier mâché and set about first imitating and then developing the exotic oriental lacquered furniture that was to blossom and flourish in the Georgian and Victorian periods.

The simplest example of papier mâché that you could find would be a schoolboy's 'spitball': a small wad of exercise-book paper lovingly chewed and moulded into a deadly missile for his catapult; papier mâché means 'mashed or chewed paper' and it may be that the French émigré workers (from whom we get the word), working in the papier mâché shops in London during the eighteenth century, really did prepare the paper by chewing it for moulding small objects. Certainly, manufacturers did nothing to discourage the popularity of this idea, as it helped to shroud in mystery exactly how they did prepare their papier mâché. So jealously guarded were their methods of preparation that even today we know only that papier mâché was made with a binder of glue or gum arabic, flour, sawdust, resin, wax and plaster, or combinations of these with probably other ingredients that we know nothing of.

A manufacturer named John Baskerville, known for his fine books and typefounding, in about 1740 began successfully imitating the lacquered papier mâché pieces from Japan and subsequently this lacquering technique was known as 'japanning'. His assistant, Henry Clay, invented a method of preparing papier mâché that was not only stronger than wood but virtually heat-proof. Paper pulp was mixed with glue or gum arabic and the pulp stream kneaded and passed through rollers to achieve a slab of uniform thickness. This was dried slowly at a low temperature to prevent warping. The panels that he moulded from papier mâché were made up of ten or more sheets of soft, unsized paper, both sides of each sheet pasted with a mixture of boiled glue and flour and laid into a mould; this was drenched in linseed oil and dried at a temperature of 38°C (100°F). They were then ready to be used as panels for ceilings and partitions. They were extremely popular for all types of wheeled carriages, being light, strong and resilient.

When Henry Clay's patent expired many small firms sprang up, centred mainly in Birmingham and Wolverhampton, and the production of virtually everything from buttons to beds began in earnest. It is from these firms we get the beautiful, rich, black enamel papier mâché, gilded and decorated with flakes of mother of pearl. These flakes were softened, cut to shape and laid in position on the piece to be decorated; the thick, black varnish was built up in layers around it. This black varnish was a mixture of amber,

Writing case with mother-of-pearl inlay

Chair, circa 1850

linseed oil, resin and asphaltum thinned with turpentine: asphaltum was a bitumous substance coming from the Dead Sea and commonly known as 'Jewish glue'.

'Jenners and Bettridge' is the name we associate with this period: a Birmingham firm boasting shops in London and New York, it produced papier mâché objects of superb quality and decoration which are now largely museum pieces.

By 1860 the production of papier mâché reached a degree of perfection that precluded it from being used as a material for the new mass-production techniques; manufacturers were impatient to cater more speedily to a growing wealthier section of the population. They turned their attention to laminated wood, iron, plaster and plastic and, suddenly, papier mâché was out of fashion. A contributing factor to the rapid decline may have been that the new dresses of the day, with their starched and heavy underskirts, would simply send the lightweight chairs and small tables flying. Social mishaps like these would not have to occur very often before the offending pieces would be removed to the servants' rooms or nursery, never to return.

In any event, the great days of papier mâché were over, and japanners took their skills over to the new car and bicycle industries.

The Victoria Regina cot. Designed for Jenners and Betteridge, magnificently ugly, but a good example of papier mâché dexterity in its heyday

Papier mâché has had a rather more virile recent history in America. Perhaps there is something in the American temperament that is more in tune with the versatility of papier mâché, which is a very lively art/craft medium there today.

Papier mâché was first introduced to America by one William Allgood, a Northamptonshire Quaker and a leading expert in japanning. He started the highly successful Litchfield Manufacturing Company, remembered now for its richly decorated clock cases. Papier mâché survived not so much as a trade, as it had in England, but as a craft, taken up by women to provide themselves with all manner of useful and decorative household objects, developing their skills in papier mâché very much as they had done in their quilt work. The art of papier mâché was given a boost in the 1960s by a successful artist/designer, called Gemma, from New York, working with her husband in Mexico. Although her work there bore no relation to the traditional Mexican papier mâché which had long been used for making festival decorations, masks and traditional dolls, she attracted the interest of Mexican artists, who emulated and were later taught by her, with her beautiful applied papier mâché. From this a thriving industry has developed with a strong following in the United States.

15

Again in America, papier mâché is being applied to existing objects, mostly furniture, giving new life to things which would otherwise be discarded. This, coupled with the sophisticated use of modern materials, like automobile enamels for giving perfect and durable finishes, is a lovely instance of combining the best of the old with the best of the new.

In the heyday of papier mâché there were men like Isaac Weld, an Irishman from County Cork, who in 1800 made a boat from papier mâché and sailed it on the lakes of Killarney; and in 1833 Charles Frederick Bielefeld built ten prefabricated cottages and a ten-roomed villa for transportation to Australia at the request of a client for his party to inhabit instantly on arrival. This papier mâché village could be assembled in just four hours.

Charles Bielefeld's prefabricated papier mâché house, taken from a drawing which appeared in the Illustrated London News *in 1853. The rest of his houses were rather more utility. This must have been the absolute minimum that a Victorian gentleman of means considered tolerable living quarters. The inside was as handsomely appointed as the outside*

The disappointment that men like Weld and Bielefeld would feel if they were unlucky enough to come back and witness the dwindling away to near non-existence in England of this easy-going medium can only be guessed at; particularly in the face of the staggering production (not to say waste) of paper today. (It is a sobering thought that for one edition of a Sunday newspaper sixteen acres of forests are used.) All this and the tremendous range of acrylics, epoxies, polyurethanes, varnishes, lacquers, enamels and spray paints, the possibilities of which would have simply made them weak at the knees.

Perhaps a latter-day Charles Bielefeld will introduce papier mâché for building again, using our over-abundance of waste paper, possibly for building on known earth-tremor lines; the paper would absorb vibration as no other material could. Alternatively, instant and moderately durable buildings could be made, to be helicoptered into disaster areas, or the bodywork of lightweight electric cars for cities (papier mâché was used for the nose cones of fighter planes during the last war), and so on.

With the clever new machines that we have taught to do our daily work for us in a matter of seconds, dealing with the resulting increase in leisure time is proving an embarrassing problem. Papier mâché is one craft we can take up and one which may find itself precisely in step with the times again. It is tempting to write a long list of its virtues; enough to say that it is wonderfully good-natured stuff, due for a renaissance.

Setting up a work area

The minimum you need is really no more than a quiet corner of your own somewhere near a window, with a table, a chair and a light placed on either side of you, shielded in such a way that at no time do you glimpse a naked bulb. A wooden box about 60 cm (2 ft) square enables you to vary the height of the model and work from more than one viewpoint.

Perfect for modelling heads on, is a piece of dowel rod or broom handle about 1 m (3 ft) long. Resting on the ground and gripped between your knees, it revolves easily and leaves both hands free to work.

Work near a window but not facing it, and only paint with colour by daylight, when this is possible. Models painted by electric light can look disappointingly washed out in daylight and those painted by fluorescent light can look horribly crude and overblown next morning.

Keep the working surface clean; rummaging for small tools hidden under the paper spoils the concentration. A large cardboard box beside you encourages you to throw paper away the moment it is finished with.

A small layout pad is the best palette; simply tear off the leaves as they get used up.

If your scissors or knives are blunt then treat yourself to some new ones. If they are not razor sharp they are likely to cause a lot of damage to the model.

You also need a bucket of water and an old towel to rinse your hands in frequently: fingers get sticky and uncomfortable and then, just as you get a piece of paper modelled perfectly in place, you could find that it has preferred to stay stuck to your finger.

Whether you work alone or with other people around is up to you, of course. Sometimes people can say just the right thing at the right time, giving us a whole new surge of interest when we had had just about enough; but whatever they say can be useful, even when it's obvious that they are missing the point.

Stop to clean and clear everything on the table occasionally – if you don't, a moment may come when you feel that everything is slipping out of control.

A note before starting

You may feel quite secure in the knowledge that you're *not* going to start, thank you very much, having just flicked through the book and seen page after page of instructions. If you have enough application to make a Christmas cake or take a carburettor to pieces then you can take a model through its various stages to a successful completion.

I will tell you why I say this.

Working with papier mâché this way uses two memories – that of sight and that of touch. We all know what things 'look' like and 'feel' like because we notice things and handle things all day long. Since childhood we have been building up this stockpile of impressions of how skin and hair, leather, stone, fabric and china, etc, look and feel. Modelling like this triggers off these two memories, and I notice that what happens is that most people, time and time again, surprise themselves at the skill that they can bring to bear on the making of their model. It is these two memories coming into play. Hitherto, since we hadn't had

20

a great deal of need for them, we were largely unconscious that they were there at all.

I am not saying that this work is easy but I *am* saying that you have a lot more going for you than you think and you won't know this until you start.

Modelling for children

Children take to this type of modelling with paper like professionals. You might think that they had done it all their lives. Adults tend to be more tentative, using the papier mâché at first as though it were clay, but children bash straight in, quite fearless. They appreciate the speed at which the whole thing works, the range of effects that they can get; if well organized, they will start a model in the morning and take it home finished at teatime. It *does* need organizing, because they tend to get excited and race ahead. A good introduction is to get them to start by making finger or glove puppets, such as clowns, witches and wizards, frogs, old ladies and gentlemen, kings and queens, very fat men, goats, octopuses, soldiers, cooks, birds, crocodiles, devils.

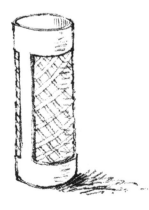

Buy some plastic hair curlers from Woolworths or your local general store. These come in three sizes and the two smaller sizes fit children's fingers: being aertex, they simply couldn't be more perfectly designed, allowing the puppet to dry from the inside.

A wooden block about 7·5 cm by 10 cm by 5 cm (3 in by 4 in by 2 in) should be available for each child, with a wooden peg (or large nail, made thicker by binding some rag around it) protruding about 5 cm (2 in) above the block set near one end to act as a prop. If you are not able to provide these modelling aids, the neck of a small beer or medicine bottle is almost as good. Slip the hair curler over one end of this and pad it with a little scrap of paper to stop it wobbling about. Tissue paper and Polycell should be prepared and ready (shown on page 39). Children should be shown how to make the tissue paper into wads (page 42). When they have made a few wads and got the hang of it, making them neither too dry nor too wet and soggy, they then can start building up a ball on the hair curler. The first few wads are put on and then, to stop these dropping straight off again, make some small lengths of doubled tissue pieces about 6 cm ($2\frac{1}{2}$ in) long and crisscross them over the wads like pieces of elastoplast. Continue adding these wads and securing them when necessary.

Children should start modelling the puppet's nose quite early on so they know the front of the head from the back; encourage them not to make the back of the head too flat. The nose should be good and firm, as should be the whole head. (See section on Heads, page 73.)

Get them to stop at a certain point and clean up, continuing more slowly and carefully as they model up the features. Ears can be pieces of tissue trebled and squashed flat, shaped by folding, and 'elastoplasted' into place. They do tend to drop off.

When complete, dry the heads over with a very hot current of air until the surface tissue is brittle.

They may want to add more detail, or if not they can paint them with emulsion using it as a 'filler' rather than as a paint.

A good two hours' drying is needed now until the head is firm and too hard for accidental damage. The children either should go out to play or, if keen to go on, make the hands, if it is a glove puppet, by cutting a hair curler into three parts and using two pieces to model the hands over

23

(illustrated alongside). There are also hats to prepare, plus hair, glasses (see page 77), walking sticks, and other accessories.

As large as possible a range of 'hair' should be available – coarse string, wool, wood shavings, wire wool, felt, rag, raffia, fur, straw, anything. Polystyrene is useful to have about, as is self-hardening modelling clay. Also cork, sand, dried peas (for warts). The simplest glove for the puppet could be made from a handkerchief with holes cut at the right places for the head and hands, with lace and jewellery, etc, stuck on as appropriate.

Some finger puppets are very effective in a play if the operator wears a neutral-coloured glove and if the head, with little or no neck, is just stuck on the end of a finger.

A play might arise quite naturally out of the varied characters and animals created, and that might be more enterprising than making puppets for an existing play.

Once children can see the number of things that can be made, they will usually provide their own ideas after that; although only one or two may ever go on to develop this papier mâché work, it will always remain a useful item in their repertoire of 'how to make things'.

A small group of six-year-olds from the Rudolph Steiner School, Edinburgh. New to this type of modelling they managed to get the heads modelled in two hours. After the models were dried and emulsioned overnight the children painted and finished them off in two hours the following afternoon. Children should have a wide variety of things to choose from for making clothes, hair and accessories. They work at such an enthusiastic speed that they can get frustrated if they cannot carry out their ideas instantly

Glove puppet

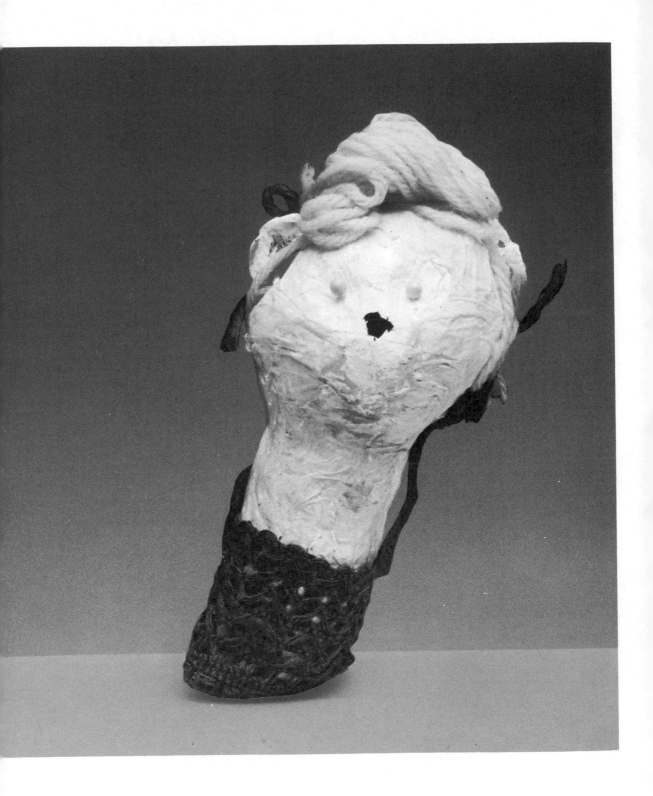

The duet: piano made from polystyrene, curved slightly to give a false perspective; ornamentation is plaster-soaked bandage, dried peas and a christmas card

33

Master and mistress: two eighteenth-century figures.
Most of the references for this modelled scene come from Hogarth's
Marriage à la Mode. Note that paintings and drawings from the
period tend to make more authoritative sources of reference than later
reconstructions. As he is depicting his own period the artist puts in
observations that a later artist, thinking them odd and unnecessary,
might edit out.

The figures and their settings were made up as follows:
Fireplace: polystyrene, drinking straws, dried peas and modelling clay
Drapes: good quality linen, stiff enough for the folds not to collapse
when wet with paste, in this case a policeman's shirt was used
Frame: thin cord and very thin strips of bandage soaked in plaster of
Paris

Master: wig – strands of floor mop; scarf – tissue paper; coat and shoes – thick brown paper; stockings and waistcoat – typing paper
Mistress: hair – copper strands of fuse wire; dress – tissue paper

Carpet: velvet daubed with emulsion
Grate (detail): card, matchsticks,
modelling clay and real coal (one of
the few things that looks as real in
miniature as normal size)
Dogs: modelling clay

Mantelpiece (detail): books from
card and tissue paper; Staffordshire
dog from modelling clay, varnished

Making a model

From the start we need a clear idea of the model we want. Usually better ideas occur to us as we work and we can alter the model as we go along.

Start with a figure plus some small related objects:

an old lady, blown along by a terrific wind
a clown balancing crockery on a pole
a fat gentleman sitting on a shooting stick
a witch cooking something horrible in a pot
a chef carrying an enormous wedding cake (about to trip
    over a sleeping cat)
a Scotsman playing bagpipes
a lady wearing a huge flowered hat and lacy summer
    dress
a model of yourself, wearing the clothes you have on at
    the moment

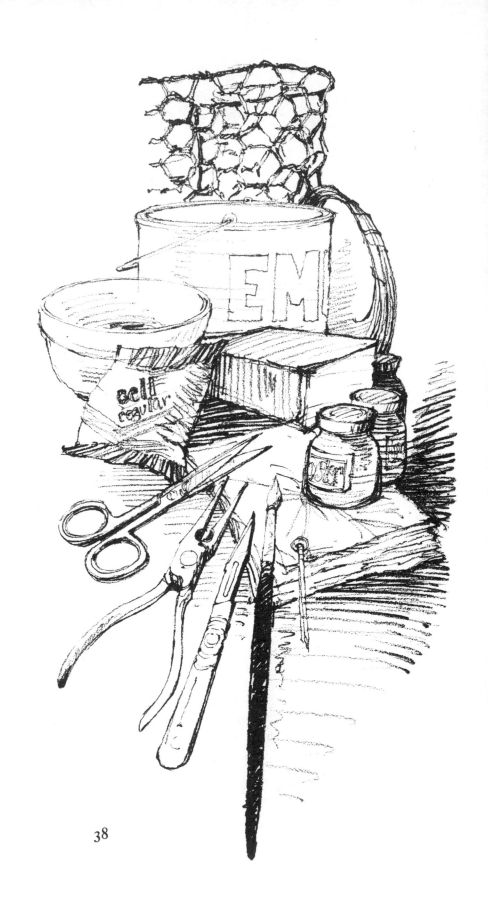

Tools and materials

Most of these may be in the house already:

small packet of Polycell wallpaper paste
pudding bowl or plastic dish
block of wood about 10 cm by 15 cm by 5 cm (4 in by
   6 in by 2 in)
one large nail, hammer, a metre (3 ft) of thin wire, a pair
   of electrician's pliers and a pair of sharp scissors
three packets of white tissue paper and six sheets of
   typing paper
a little plasticine or self-hardening modelling material
some small-gauge chicken wire, about twice the size of
   this book
a small paint brush, five pots of poster paint (basic
   colours), some white emulsion and a small tin of
   varnish
a small table vice is useful, but not essential
a scalpel is invaluable

Directions

Sprinkle half the Polycell into 0.25 litres (half a pint) of
water in the bowl. Stir. Five minutes later stir again. Leave
for at least twenty minutes.

Meanwhile, bang the nail firmly into the block of wood,
just off-centre. This will be one leg of the model and may
need to go in at a slight angle according to the model's pose.

*Hammer in the nail at a slight angle,
but not so deep that it cannot be
prised out later*

Armature

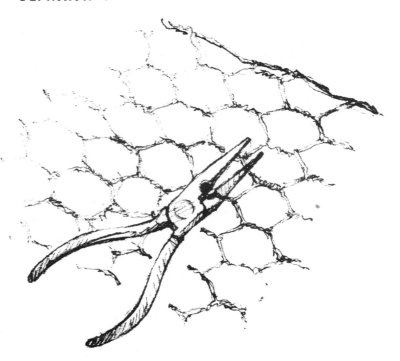

Cut the wire where it is doubled

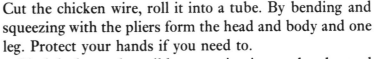

Cut the chicken wire, roll it into a tube. By bending and squeezing with the pliers form the head and body and one leg. Protect your hands if you need to.

Bind the leg to the nail by wrapping it round and round the nail, not allowing the ankle to become too thick.

Cut 23 cm (9 in) of thin wire and secure it to the shoulders, having two lengths extended as arms. Add a length to the hip for the second leg.

It does not matter how rough it looks as long as it is fairly firm and has the shape of the figure.

Spend some time now, twisting and bending this armature into a good, exaggerated and characteristic pose.

Note: if I say that the armature is not too important there will be some raised eyebrows. Obviously, nobody can work with an armature so ill-made that it flops over or falls to bits but, when the armature is covered in papier mâché and dried, it has no further function than to secure the arms to the body and the body to the stand – the dried papier

40

mâché will be stronger than the armature anyway. Also, one of the advantages of this method is that we can alter, at any time, the position of our figure. He can stand up or sit down, bend over, raise one arm or another until we find a really telling posture. Too solid an armature may inhibit this plasticity, and, lastly, armatures are not very interesting, so why waste time on them?

Making the armature was one of the worst jobs, as sore fingers will testify, but now it is finished. Tear the tissue paper into 10 cm by 5 cm (4 in by 2 in) pieces and stack it into a pile next to the paste, which by now is like jelly. Lightly scoop a little paste on the tips of three fingers of your writing hand and pick up the top tissue.

Fold it and screw it, using both hands, into a fairly tight ball or pad and press firmly on to the chest of the model. The idea is that we want the tissue paper pasted only in patches. As we fold and screw the paper it picks up paste from the fingers in some places but not in others: too much paste and the tissue paper becomes sodden and slimy; too little and the screwed ball begins to spring open again.

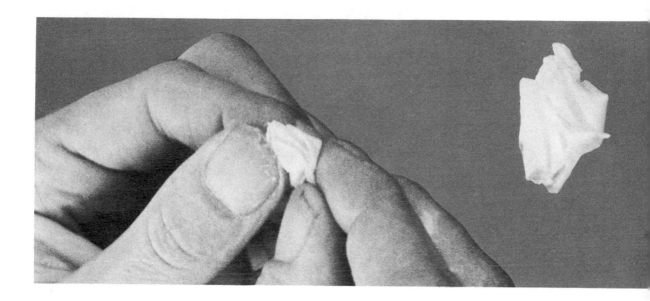

This process of making the tips of the fingers sticky and folding and screwing the paper into an untidy ball or pad is the basic motion of preparing tissue paper to build up the model. We build and add and smooth off, working round the figure, building up the shape. If the model feels too wet, add pieces of drier tissue. If too dry, pieces will fall off. Secure these by putting glued strips over them, like strips of elastoplast.

Take longer pieces of tissue and wind them bandage-fashion around the arms and legs, letting the paper take up glue from the fingers in the same way. Keep the model's wrists and ankles thin. The hands are made separately. Do not put too much definition in the head for the moment. Just indicate the eye sockets, nose and chin.

The model has probably reached a point where it needs to dry now. Put it on the plate rack of a gas stove over a gas flame that is not fierce, but not too gentle either; being very wet it won't catch on fire. A blow heater is also good. The model dries best in a current of hot air. Radiators are too slow except for overnight drying. The inside of the model takes some days to dry, so be content if after half an hour over the gas the surface of the model is dry and hard enough to continue working on.

Hands

While the figure dries, make its hands. Take ten pieces of tissue 1.5 cm by 2.5 cm (3 in by 1 in). Fold as in the diagram with your fingers only lightly pasted. Of the ten fingers made, choose the two thickest for thumbs, and place four fingers each next to the thumbs. Use your own hand as a guide to which finger is longer than another. Take care not to make two left or two right hands.

44

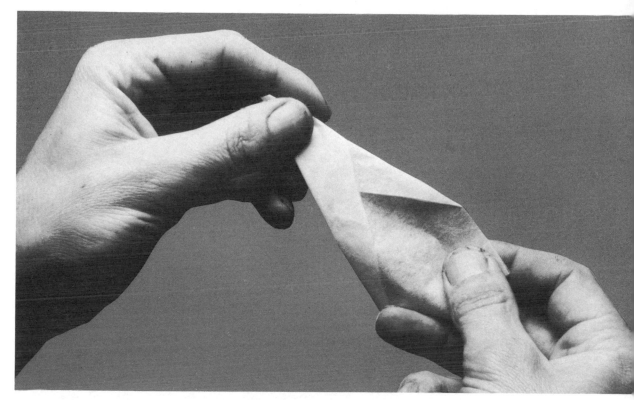

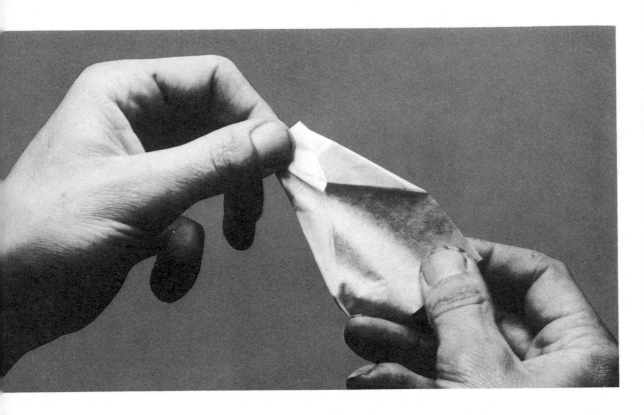
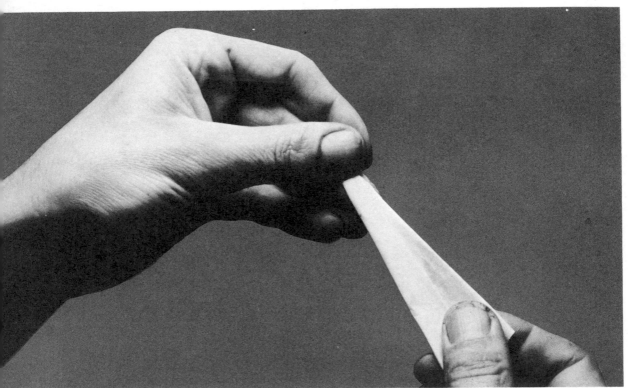

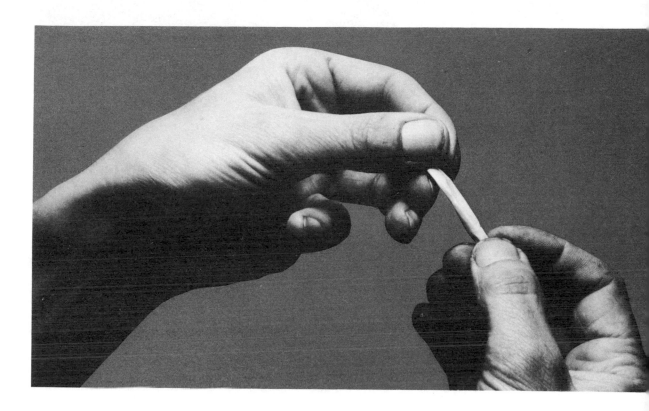

Take these five fingers in your hand and wrap sticky tissue around the base of the knuckles and between the thumb. Don't attempt to shape the fingers too much now or they may begin to come apart. Hang over the gas to dry. Let the two hands become semi-dry before shaping. If the hand is too bulky when clenched, snip off the tops of the fingers or cut one finger out entirely. Bind the hands to the model's wrist with more sticky tissue. They may look rather large. If so, it is all to the good. Slightly oversized hands often suit a model.

If these hands still look wrong, just leave them. You can work on them later.

Model the front and back of the head at the same time.

Use the tissue in the same way as before but now in much smaller pieces. A nail file or small knife is useful for pressing and smoothing surfaces. Eyes set well back in their sockets are shadowed and more alive.

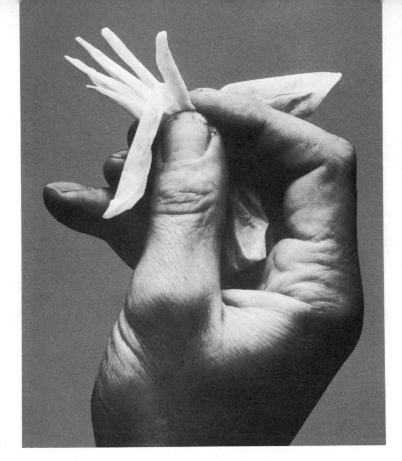

Securing the thumb

Hand ready for drying

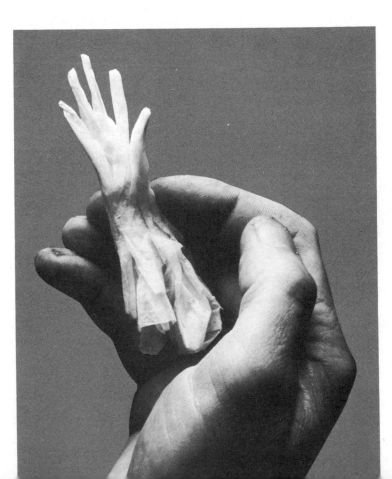

The chapter on Heads, page 73, may be of some help.

We should now have the head modelled, hands in position and feet shaped.

Dry for an hour.

When dry the model has probably become wrinkled and stained. In fact it looks so incredibly dreary and disappointing that you may feel like strangling it. Do, and at the same time remind it that if it wasn't for you it would still be just a few old bits of waste paper lying about; they soon toe the line after that, you'll find. You are about halfway to finishing, and if the first half wasn't much fun, the second more than makes up for it.

Next you become a tailor and need a sharp pair of scissors and some typing or exercise-book paper. Good-quality writing paper may be too stiff. Dress the model in the same order as that which it would have used if it had dressed itself that morning.

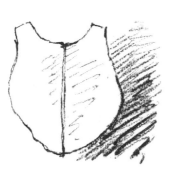

Shirt front

Cut out the shirt front from typing paper with a crease down the centre (it looks like a waiter's dickie), and paste it firmly on to the model's breast.

Collar and cuffs

Take the neck measurement with a piece of cotton. Cut out the collar shape. Smear the inside with paste. Fold. Smear the neck of the model and press the collar into place. Put on the cuffs in the same way.

Trousers

Cut out each leg, paste it and crease. Paste the leg and press on the trouser so that the crease comes to the front and untidy joins go to the back. Move trousers about as little as possible once they are on. Keep any folds that look natural, smooth out any that don't. Cut out a new pair of trousers if the first pair need too much adjusting and have lost their crispness.

Waistcoat

Cut out the shape. Paste inside the waistcoat and the model's chest and press in place. Pull the waistcoat taut across the tummy if the model is fat.

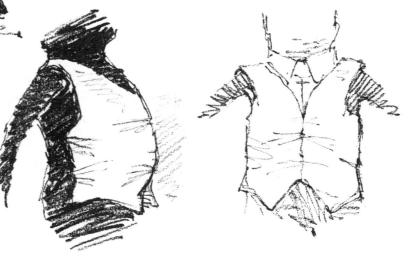

Jacket

Work on the sleeves first; they go almost over the cuffs at one end and are moulded to the shoulders at the other. If the arm is very bent, straighten it, add the sleeve and gently

bend it back. If it is very close to the body, wait until the rest of the jacket is on before bending back into position.

Stick two pieces of typing paper together by brushing them evenly and lightly with the paste and press the two sticky sides together, squeezing out any air bubbles.

You need to cut three separate pieces for the jacket. The complete back and the left and right front. Leave out the collar and lapels for the moment and mark out the three separate pieces for the jacket. Cut them out with *sharp* scissors.

Score a line alongside, and very close to, all the outside edges with a ballpoint pen. This indentation in the soft paper will suggest a seam and although it seems a lot of extra bother for a very small result, it does take away the utility look of the clothes, playing its part later in the exquisiteness of the finished model.

Smear the body of the model and the insides of the jacket panels with a little of the paste and place all three lightly in position. Press them firmly only when you are satisfied

51

that they all hang correctly. Blend the three pieces into one complete jacket by smoothing over the joins.

Take a moment or two to slightly curl some of the jacket's edges in such a way as to give them a 'well-worn' look. With this small consideration we add another dimension to the model – time.

Paste small pieces of typing paper over any nasty gaps. Allow the bottom of the jacket to hang away from the body and flap outwards or backwards as a real one would if a person were in motion.

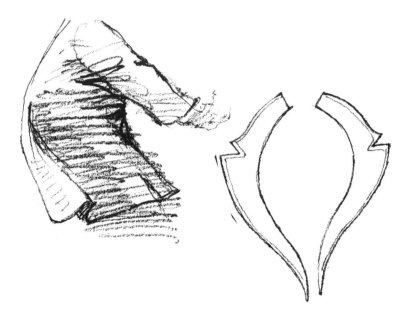

Dry for a quarter of an hour if the pieces look insecure.

Add the collar and lapels in two pieces, as shown, plus pocket flaps, ties, handkerchiefs, etc.

Hats

By now, you are better able to judge what paper to use. Very thin card would work for a top hat or a wide hat brim. Build the hat up on the head, adding hair afterwards.

Cloaks and skirts

These are made up in sections. It helps to push thin pieces of wood or wire into the model to support the cloak or skirt as it dries. It is worth taking trouble to get the feeling of movement, particularly with the old lady in the wind. (Has she a tight hold on her hat? Are we treated to a glimpse of petticoat?)

Pre-shaped and pre-folded pieces of doubled typing paper pressed on to the pasted model. Temporary pieces of wire or wood will hold them in position while they dry, when they can then support their own weight

To suggest heavy folds that reach the ground (such as period dresses or heavy curtains) take the pre-shaped piece of paper and, just before pressing it into place on the model, sharply tap it once on the table whilst holding it upright, and so force in creases at its base

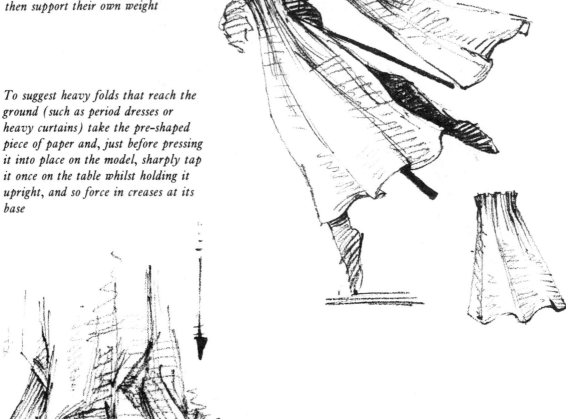

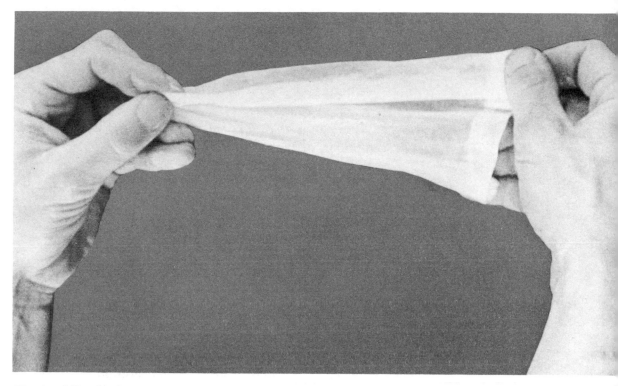

Shaping folds of a dress prior to pressing it on to the model

Props

Self-hardening modelling material is perfect for small extras like the chef's cake, the cat, crockery, etc. Plasticine is all right but needs gluing into position with Evo-Stik or Copydex.

Odd effects

Use a paper doily smeared with paste for a summer dress or parasol. Dried and split peas, rice and lentils glued on make a good texture. Tiny electrical components always seem to come in useful, as do seeds and burrs, pieces of broken fountain pen and odd bits of jewellery. Woolworths nearly always seem to have just what you need; you are going to paint the model with white emulsion, it will be impossible to tell from what these various items were originally made.

The model should be dried again now, in a warm air current overnight.

Clean away any sticky bits of tissue paper from the table and floor, or they will dry like rock.

Painting

With a soft No 6 or No 8 brush, preferably an inexpensive ox-hair one, paint the model with white emulsion. You are not really *just* painting, you are using the emulsion, which is quite thick, to fill up gaps, to smooth off surfaces that have wrinkled in the drying, and to blend one piece of the model to another. In some places the wrinkles may have been lucky accidents, for instance around the eyes or mouth, so give them just one thin coat. The jacket or dress usually needs several coats before a clean smooth surface begins to appear. It is unwise to paint the face too heavily, as the detail gets drowned. Hands usually need plenty of filling. When dry, after an hour or so over the gas, the model really looks fresh and 'together'. In fact you are definitely beginning to feel much better about the whole thing.

With fine sandpaper gently smooth off places like the nose, forehead and cheeks.

Throughout history, hardly anybody has painted on top of sculpture successfully. After we have painted ours we will probably see why. The difficulty comes if you consider the 'colouring' separately from the 'modelling'. They have to work together, with the modelling going so far and the colour taking over from there. Unless you are sensitive to this you'll just get 'painted sculpture' or, even worse, painting working *against* the sculpture and so giving a contradictory effect. Painting, in this case, is largely tinting and suggesting, especially in the face.

(To put it bluntly, it is the difference between the make-up of a beautiful and natural woman and that of a blousey old stripper.)

Start with the face. Add poster or water colour to white emulsion to get a light, warm, creamy ochre, the colour of a very light-brown chicken egg, and paint all the exposed skin areas, including the hands. Leave to dry. Meanwhile mix up plenty of colour for the jacket, trousers, dress, etc, and paint them from all angles. Paint the back of the model as thoroughly as the front. If the face is now dry, mix a delicate watery pink and lay the model on its back while you paint on this tint. As one wash dries add more to the nose, cheeks and ears. If your wash is too pink your model will have apoplexy. A good pink is obtained with crimson and yellow cooled down with the tiniest touch of green. Painting the face has to be done as delicately as possible. Don't forget the hands.

It is rare that anyone can paint something perfectly the first time, particularly large areas like coats and dresses. So, if you are not happy, mix up more colour and paint on top. (If you let tiny specks of the original colour show through, it tends to make the second colour less flat, more alive, and the contrast is too minute to be noticeable.)

A can of gold spray is very helpful. You can mask off the face and hands with tissue paper, and spray the dress gold, painting a pattern on top when dry, or give the finished painted model a very, very light spray, masking off unsuitable areas. If painting black, add crimson – it makes the black richer. Use paint thickly as this helps to get clean edges where one colour comes up against another. Painting hair is usually done best with several washes of similar colour. With a fine brush add details like eyebrows, moustaches, patterns on ties and dresses, buttons, etc.

Finally – if you have some varnish (picture varnish is best) put a dab on the nose and cheeks if it suits them to be shiny and varnish boots and shoes, or buttons and belts, or hair, but don't thoughtlessly varnish the *whole* model or most of its delicacy will disappear and it will simply look wooden.

I hope that you feel like adding a lot of extras. It is this detail that delights people who see it later, as they feel that they have discovered it for themselves. Everything we add tells more and more about the figure; he has odd socks on, for example, or pens and pencils, or a pipe in his top pocket, a handkerchief half in and half out of his pocket, or his tie is slack.

Clean off the base and sandpaper it. Varnish or paint flat black. If it is too scruffy, cut a new base and drill in a nail-size hole. Half fill the hole with glue. Carefully prise the nail and model from its old stand and drop it into the new hole. Position and support the model whilst the glue dries.

If the model was a success there is a section on page 97 which deals with making a stand and a glass case to protect it from its worst enemy, dust.

1 *Wire armature with the desk cut from featherlite board (available from some good art suppliers, used mainly for architectural models). Note that some of the surfaces are slightly curved to soften and integrate the desk with the model*

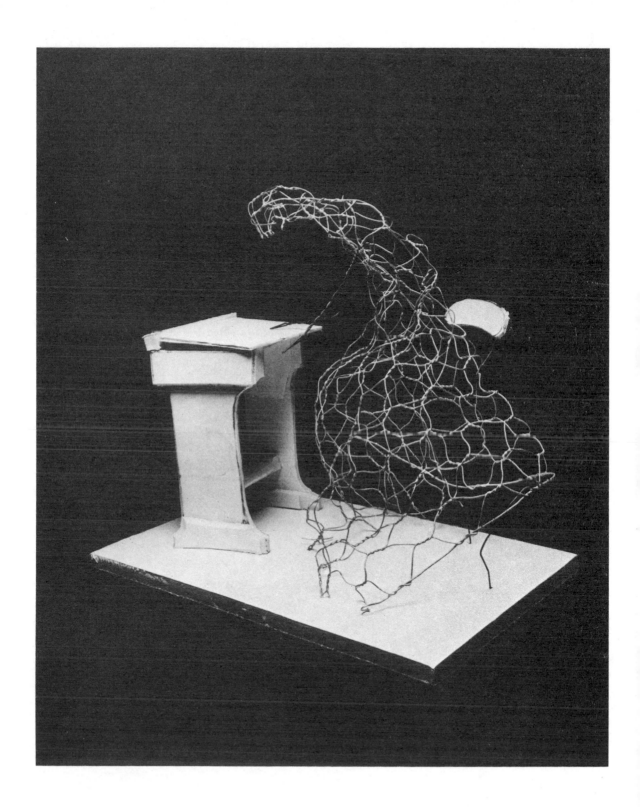

60

2   *Dress made of typing paper.*
Paper doilies were used to give some
texture to the desk and then heavily
coated in emulsion. Cat made of
modelling clay

3   *The dress was given three or four*
coats of emulsion to give it the feel of
heavy, good-quality material, the
final coat being a faded-pink colour.
The hair is of strands of double tissue
wound round the end of a fine paint
brush and pulled out slightly like a
spring. The desk is tinted with
watered-down coloured inks and the
finished model spattered with gold
spray (this spattering effect is
achieved by barely depressing the little
plastic spray unit on top of the can so
that it works inefficiently. Practise
first)

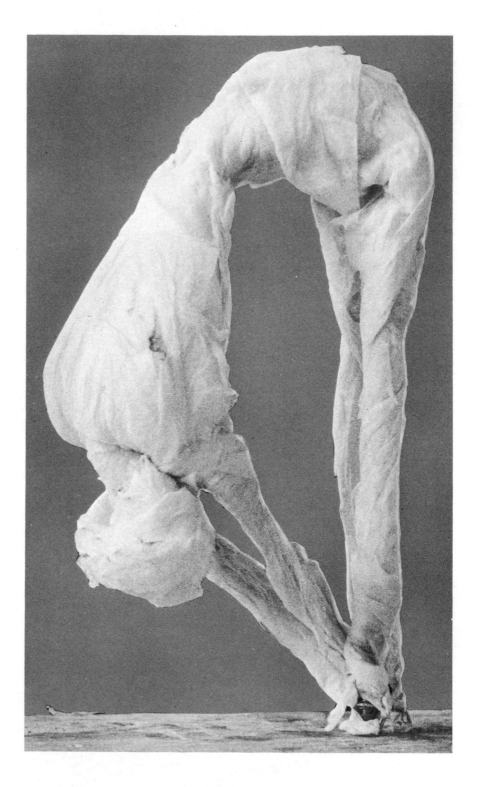

Figure at a stage where it can be tempting to give up. Usually drying it thoroughly is the answer

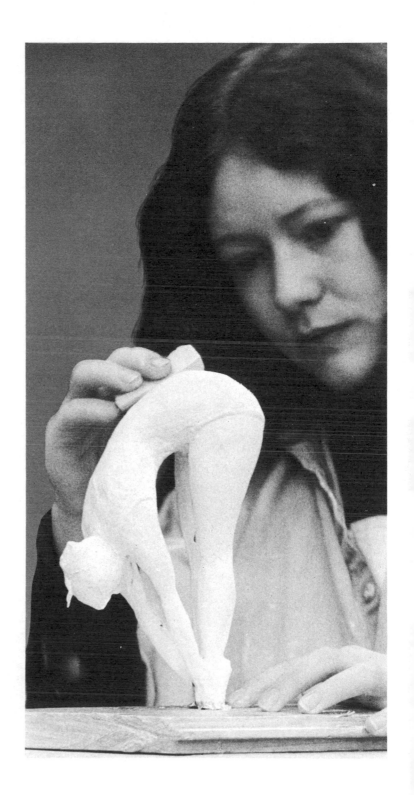

Dress from typing and tissue paper

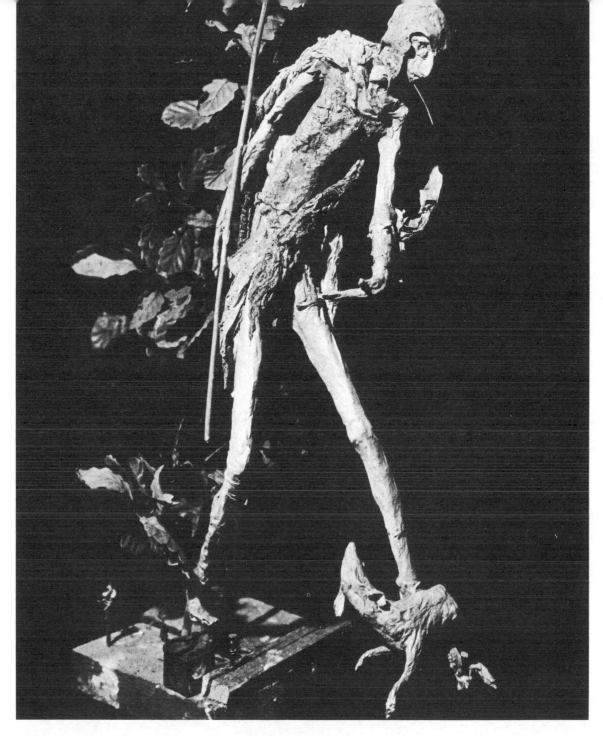

Nun on horseback, made of tissue and typing paper

Soldier kicking dog. Finished model painted with ferrous oxide and left outside to rust. Background made of real beech leaves

*Ballet figure. Legs and face sanded
down with fine sandpaper, painted
with emulsion, and sanded again*

Beau: with a knitting needle stick

Lord Longford dripping with slime (model first appeared in the Sunday Telegraph Magazine)

Idi Amin (model first appeared in the Sunday Telegraph Magazine)

Victorian hamster: modelled in tissue paper with clothes of typing paper

Life-size Jersey cow: chicken wire on a wooden frame; skin – brown paper and a velveteen tablecloth; eyes – rubber ball cut in two halves

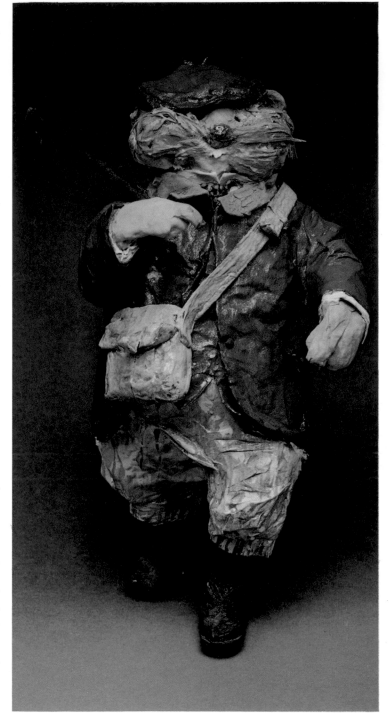

72

Modelling heads

Shape the chicken wire as shown alongside – leaving a small piece of wire extended to take the nose.

Start with a hard triangular wad of sticky tissue paper for the nose and make this the right size and shape now, if possible, so that it doesn't have to be altered later. This gives you something to 'key' the face on to and helps you begin visualizing the face in your mind's eye.

Model the face along the lines illustrated here – which roughly follow the muscles of the face.

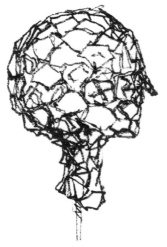

Armature

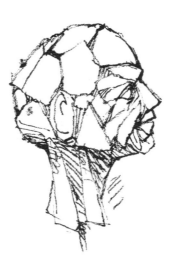 

A rough guide to follow in building up the face muscles

Set the eye sockets well back in the head and try and get the 'feel' of the face you are modelling, that is, whether it is fine and pointed or bland or heavy, etc.

For bony areas such as the forehead, cheekbone and jaw, pack the tissue paper in hard tight wads. Make slightly softer lengths for muscles and finish off with very small pieces of tissue paper laid on as skin.

Be careful not to cover the whole face with this skin and so risk losing some of the modelling which may be just right as it is.

Usually the head is completed in three stages. The first stage is roughing in the whole head, including the back (don't make this too flat, by the way).

Dry the surface very quickly over a fierce flame.

The second stage is altering and adding to the head until it is close to being finished. It is then given a chance to dry over a current of hot air until there is no longer any danger of pieces dropping off. This gives you a chance to clear up and get ready for stage three which is adding detail, painting with thick emulsion where you need smoothness and with watered-down emulsion where you would like to keep the wrinkles; also, cutting and trimming with a scalpel knife.

When the emulsion is bone dry, fine down with sand-paper areas where a silky smoothness is essential. It is possible to get a finish like porcelain if you are painstaking enough.

Suggestions for tinting and colouring the head are given on page 56.

Take the advantage of the facility that this kind of modelling gives you to squeeze, elongate or flatten the head, even when it is quite near to being finished; don't be frightened of pulling the head to pieces and re-modelling if you are quite sure it hasn't developed in a way that you are happy with.

Use the emulsion as a filler to get rid of deep gaps that shouldn't be there, and even add a little Polyfilla to thicken the emulsion if necessary.

An exercise in discipline is to make yourself model the

back of the head as thoroughly as the face, so turn the model around often as you work or it will only look right from the front.

When you achieve a piece of modelling that you are particularly pleased with, don't fiddle with it, *leave it alone!*

Eyes

Eyeball and eyelid

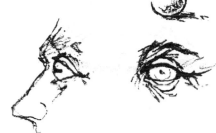

Roll out two small balls of plasticine or modelling clay and push them gently, well into the eye sockets. Two eyelid-shaped pieces above and below secure them in place. Push in two deep holes with a matchstick to make pupils and manœuvre the eyeballs so that the two eyes work together and have the right expression.

The upper eyelid should protrude well over the eyeball, throwing a shadow over the eye. Eyes can look a bit 'starey' without this.

In a smaller head it is a good idea to leave out the eyeballs altogether, leaving a deep cavity behind the eyelids; this results in the eyes being more suggestive and alive.

The corner of a piece of tissue paper pushed into the outer corner of the eye and pressed gently to the side of the head suggests beautifully the wrinkles that collect in the corner of the eye.

Two small marbles might work well for eyeballs, or pinheads pushed into the pupil, so that occasionally they just catch the light.

Mouth

As you look in the mirror you will see how your own mouth is formed and you should model a simplified version of the muscles that make it up.

Put on the teeth before making the mouth, if they are

75

to show. After modelling the mouth (illustrated alongside) put in the sheaves of muscles that lead from the outer nostril and swing out around the corner of the mouth.

If you have to alter the mouth when it has dried a little, pulling the corners up and out to make it smile or laugh, these muscles round the mouth will also stretch, and the whole area around the mouth will take up the 'laugh'.

The thing that can make models look slightly horrific is if the mouth is laughing but nothing else in the face is (like a bank manager's smile).

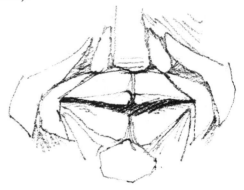

Two pieces of tissue pushed flat into the mouth and pressed against the upper and lower lip sometimes form small creases on the lips that are uncannily lifelike. Give a very sharp, clear definition to the upper lip if it is suitable for the type of face you are creating.

Hair

Putting on hair

Whatever you make the hair from, it is best put on starting from the lower back to the front of the head, the same way tiles are put on a roof.

Tissue paper can be spun into fine hair but it can get tiresome putting it on one hair at a time. It is quicker to model with large wads of tissue and only put the fine hair where it is most telling.

Cover the head well in Polycell and press the hair into it. Trim with scissors when dry.

Glasses

Pull out some strands of copper or silver wire from a piece of electric flex. Make a generous guess as to the length of wire needed and twist as many strands together as will make them up to the thickness needed for the frames. Take two of these lengths and twist them together in the centre, twist them around the handle of a paint brush or anything of the right circumference (as in the diagram); twist them together again, and bend the wire with a pair of small pliers. Insert the ends into a small hole at the ear and glue them into position. By using fine wire you get a suggestion of spectacles which is just as effective, if not more so, than modelling them in detail.

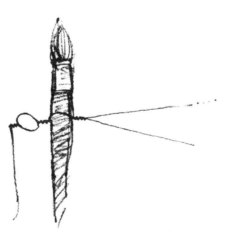

Caricature

From your experience with your first model it will be easy to appreciate how well this method of papier mâché lends itself to caricature; caricature is its nature.

Our job, then, is to try to understand a little more clearly the essence of caricature and not to get carried away by the sheer fun of exaggeration. When sitting in trains or round a table, look at a face and try to visualize it 'growing'. That is, developing forwards and backwards along the lines that the different features are already tending to go, expanding or contracting one feature at a time.

Small eyes retract to pinpricks, a domed forehead swells to a balloon. A thin small mouth becomes a hair-crack. Pink ears become fluorescent. If you can do this, even a little, it helps to break up your usual 'fixed' picture of a face into something more mobile and plastic. Then select from the four or five possibilities perhaps two around which to centre the caricature. If you try to exaggerate them all, they will tend to cancel each other out. Some features remain neutral, just playing their part in aiding the 'likeness'.

The most important overall quality that you must be aware of is the 'texture' of the person. Are they smooth, monochromed like metal, or rough and dry-textured like a cottage wall? Oily or flaky? Taut or relaxed? Neat, alert and birdlike, or an easy-going shambles? Noisy or peaceful; outward going or inward looking? This quality is likely to be echoed in line, shape, texture and colour throughout the body, from the hair to the choice of clothes, and also externally from type of furnishings right through to make of car and breed of dog.

Lastly, it would be useful to know a little about how and where the various characteristics that we know of the person display themselves. From my own observations, discrimination in a face is located at the eyebrow and the muscles that operate it. Intelligence and humour (closely related) are in the outer corner of the eye, coupled with the shadow from the eyelid. It is a pity to miss this.

The nose indicates the kind of interest a person takes in the world around him; the muscles that lead to the base of the nostrils show quite clearly a person's attitude to himself, particularly marked in self-satisfied, vain or fastidious people. Lips show how much and under what conditions a person behaves generously. Sexuality displays itself in the cheekbone and outer muscles of the neck; the chin might indicate tenacity. Seediness gives itself away at the hair behind the ear and disappointment, at the jowls. The back of the neck seems to be a display point for some characteristic that a person is largely unconscious of, possibly connected with inner growth, or lack of of it.

One last word on caricature that is worth remembering: some people find it odious. Perhaps they feel that life is quite bizarre enough already without deliberately 'aggravating' it; they may prefer quietly to overlook a person's idiosyncrasies and contradictions. Happily, many more people enjoy it, seeing their own privately formed observations confirmed.

If the caricature is truthfully, remorselessly but sympathetically done, without vindictiveness, then it embodies a good deal of truth from which everyone can learn, not

least the sitter. Features like smugness, pomposity, lewd-
ness, cunning, servility, humourlessness, indolence and the
like, need to be lampooned and it is interesting that genuine
qualities like intelligence, innocence, compassion and
courage defy parody: the joke backfires. You could try a
caricature model of yourself. That might make quite a vivid
introduction.

Methods

Essentially, the same processes are used for the caricature
as for the first model. If you choose to do a large head or
a miniature body, the placing of the nail has to be well considered beforehand, and be quite secure.

On a miniature body, the size of the hands vary according
to their position and importance, but generally speaking
they should be miniature if held at the sides, and increase
rapidly in size as they come up to the level of the face.

It is best to model the whole figure altogether, although
there is a strong temptation to model the head first and
attach a body later. When modelling the head, as in straight
portraiture, it is important to have a clear feel of the person
right from the application of the first piece of papier mâché
on to the wire armature.

When the figure is almost completely modelled but still
damp, it is then possible to manœuvre the head about radi-
cally. The nose can be pulled and extended right out, or the
head crushed downward like a toad, or the sides of the head
squeezed together. If the head has been well constructed
– that is, the muscles modelled on the same principle as
actual ones – it is possible for it to survive these distortions
(after a bit of patching up) and still be very believable as
a head; only now it will be far bolder and more extreme
than we could have visualized initially.

There is usually something that will mimic hair perfectly, coarse string combed out, wire wool, wood shavings,
etc, which may need a light painting or spraying to blend

them with the rest of the model. Use real objects where appropriate; artificial pearls, matchsticks or scalpel blades for teeth, for example, and real false eyelashes. Also, you might consider placing the figure in a historical or mythological setting. It may well 'suit' your subject to be portrayed as an eighteenth-century fop, a Pan, Boudicca, Harlequin, a Victorian explorer, etc. Particularly effective would be to metamorphize the person into a peacock or hawk; a lion, snake or mouse; even a pig!

Finish off by adding pertinent objects such as a piece of furniture, a typewriter, a miniature building, a musical instrument, golf clubs, as a final comment.

Charles de Gaulle, about 30 cm (12 in) high

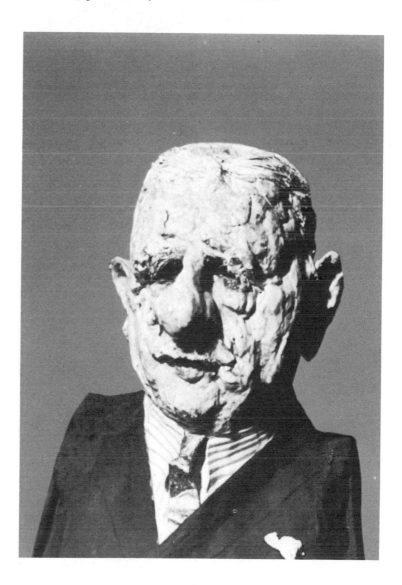

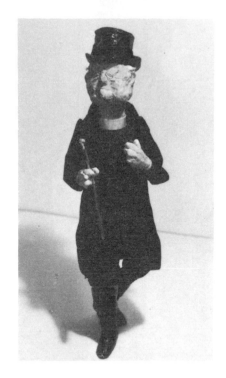

Bishop, suit made of velvet

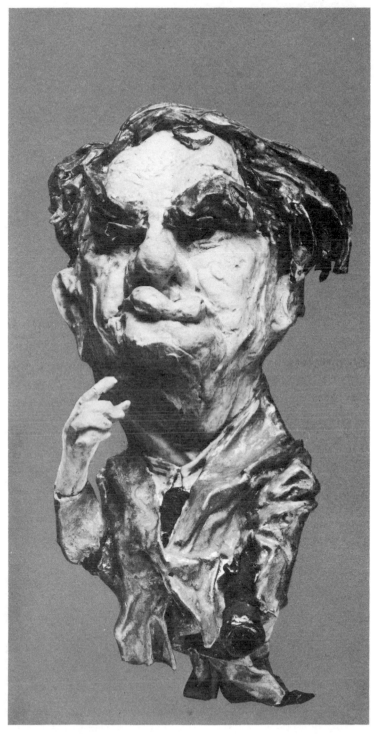

*Caricature model of Patrick Moore,
about 40 cm (16 in) high*

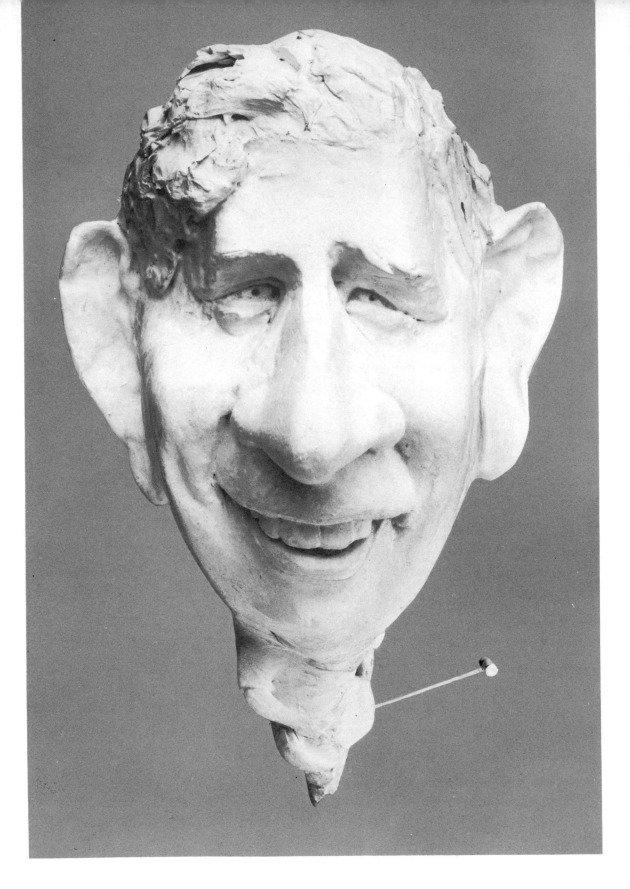

*HRH The Prince of Wales
(unpainted)*

*Vicar, 4.25 m (14 ft), modelled in
brown paper, trousers of sacking, teeth
of yellow soap*

Small caricature model of the harpist Graham Bell. The harp is cut out of polystyrene and the base made from a block of wood bound round with string, painted, and spattered with gold spray

Making animals

Armature

The method of making these animals is very similar to making a figure. The armature is best made from small-gauge chicken wire on a piece of plank about 30 cm (12 in) long with a hole drilled in the centre. A length of soft wire to support the chicken wire is fixed firmly in this hole. The wire is only to support the chicken wire and should be as simple as possible, because as you make the model you may have a much better idea for it and want to alter its position, and too well-made an armature might make this difficult. Wire coat hangers are about the right thickness but are too stiff and springy – use them if you cannot find any softer wire; the perfect thing is aluminium armature wire but this is not easy to find, except in some craft shops.

Model the animal as quickly as you can and get it into a good, lively, characteristic posture. You might like to make two animals fighting or playing – a lot more work but well worth it.

Build up the animal using tissue paper for the muscles

but where you want soft folds of loose skin use paper handkerchiefs or kitchen roll. Thin brown paper is very good for tough, wrinkled skin where the skin is flexible.

There are hundreds of things that you can use to make the animal's texture. Scales, for instance, can be made from small, stiff green leaves, from seeds, or cut from card.

A good knobby, warty effect can be got by using rice, lentils or split peas, anything like that. A hunt through the larder should produce just the right thing.

Crocodile skin can be emulated with small rough pieces of bark. These are stuck on the model by coating the animal in thick Polycell, pressing them on and allowing to dry. After they have been painted with thick emulsion it's almost impossible to see what they are so you should feel free to use anything you like, absolutely anything. Eggshells put on and gently crushed make good armoured skin. Fur can be built up with fine pieces of tissues, possibly some soft cloth, imitation-velvet or even real fur. Real fur has to be sprayed gently with spray paint several times first to make it stiff, then it can be painted with emulsion. Snake-skin can be suggested by cutting up a fine-meshed nylon 'onion-bag' and sticking pieces on. Fine sand sprinkled on to the wet glue will also work. When dry, different grasses can be ideal for making crests, plumes or whiskers.

Painting

The notes on painting a model on page 56 apply here too. When painting an animal you can be quite bold in getting the effect that you want; cans of spray paint and small jars of fluorescent poster paint are useful.

A good effect for crocodiles can be caught by polishing the finished model with light-brown boot polish. Matt varnish is another way of finishing it off. Having made your animal, put it in a natural setting such as clumps of dried grass, or a cave with bones scattered on a sandy floor.

Making large animals

This demands much the same approach as smaller animals, but everything will be proportionally larger.

The armature has to be made of light wood and so the finished model should be worked out in some detail before-hand as it will be difficult to alter later on. Larger-gauge chicken wire can be used as small-gauge wire, although better, can work out expensive. Larger wads of tissue paper can be used for the finer modelling, with thin brown paper for making muscles. Strips of newspaper make a good tight skin to build upon when thoroughly dry.

You have to use your imagination as to the variety of

textures and the materials required for them, but polystyrene is especially useful. You can cut, tear or burn the
shapes you need.

Paint the animal thickly with emulsion when dry.

The life-size cow (shown on page 72) was made in this
way, using a velveteen tablecloth for skin and some old
carrots for udders (which later unfortunately sprouted!).

Large models soon lose their freshness and get to look
very dogeared unless protected, so give them four or five
coats of varnish – the final coat being matt – particularly
if they are to go outside.

*Dinosaur, 45 cm (18 in) high.
Armoured skin is represented by
eggshells gently crushed on to the
pasted model*

90

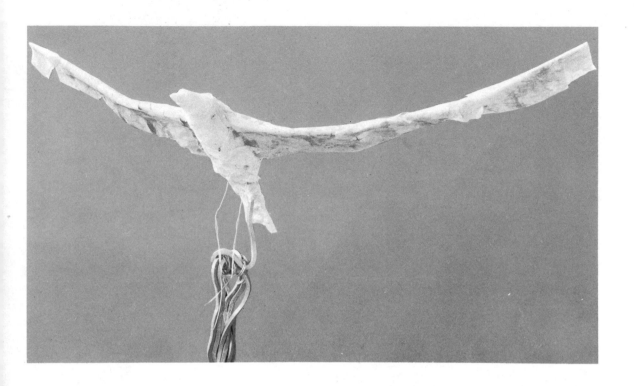

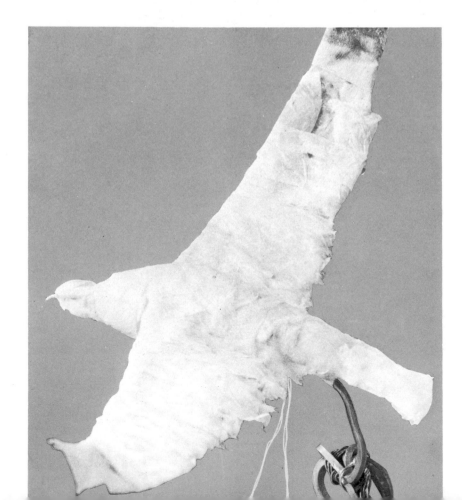

Three stages of a seagull

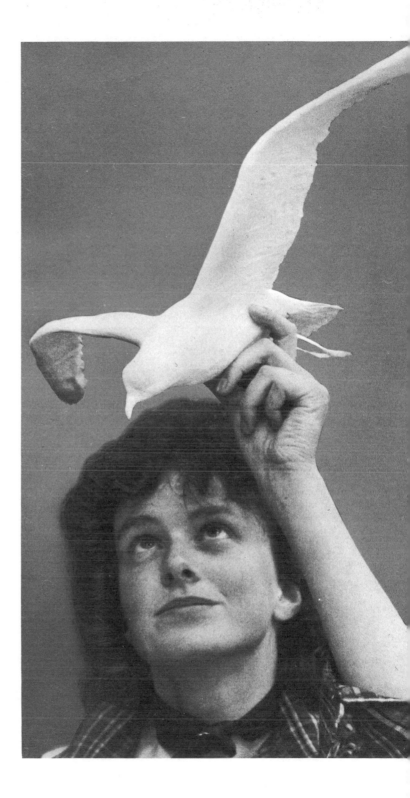

Crocodile, about 60 cm (24 in) long.
The model was thickly smeared with
paste, and encrusted with rough tree
bark, lentils, split peas and rice

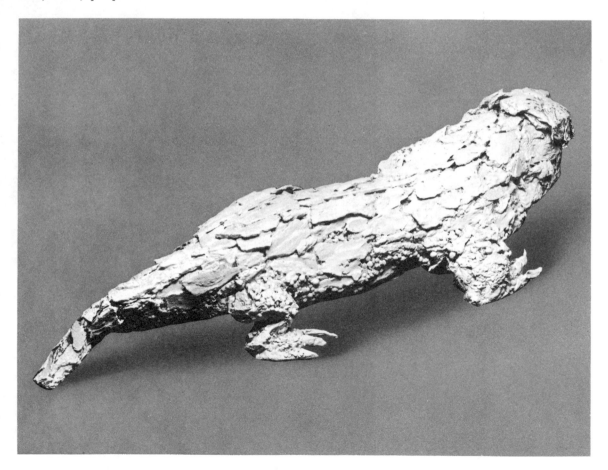

94

Making a stand

If you want to make a really posh stand for your figure go to a frame-making shop and buy a round, oval or oblong wooden frame: a really well made, good-looking stand is important. It means that you are saying to the world, 'I know it's papier mâché but I think it is a beautiful thing, capable of standing on a shelf alongside carriage clocks and Dresden china. I am proud of it, that is why I have invested money and care on the stand.' Stuck on an old lump of wood, your model will have a 'take it or leave it' sort of appearance.

Place the frame on some stout card and cut out a base. Glue the base card on to the frame with latex paper glue (Copydex). When dry, paint the whole stand inside and out with emulsion, particularly the inside where the card joins the frame.

Bend or splay the wire or nail protruding from the model so that the model will rest level with the top of the stand.

Fill in the frame with plaster of Paris – dental plaster from the chemist is best – and secure the model into position whilst it dries. You may prefer to build up the plaster on the stand into rocks or steps, whatever the model suggests. A pleasing effect for the stand is first to paint it a dark rusty red, then spray on gold paint in several even coats, and when quite dry very gently sand it with fine sandpaper, so that the red just begins to show here and there.

To make a simpler stand: keep the block of wood that the model is on already and cover the four outside edges with latex adhesive. When that is semi-dry, wind good-quality string or fine cord round and round the stand with one layer right next to another, starting at the top of the back. Paint it over with emulsion and spray gold. Clean off and polish or varnish the top.

Making a case

This is not so simple, and it is a shame that the very last job should be so difficult. Under glass a model will keep its colour and freshness for years; unprotected it will fade and, worst of all, collect dust. Even with a feather duster dust will stay in the crevices. Your model will go the way of all unprotected papier mâché and become tired-looking, dogeared and tatty which is what gives papier mâché a bad name. You may be fortunate enough to come across a glass case which is the right size or even a glass dome from a carriage clock. You can buy plastic domes for carriage clocks imported from Switzerland plus a wooden base to fit, if you know a real clock shop, but they do take some hunting down. It is most likely that you will have to make one of your own.

This requires picture glass cut very accurately (people who like the plasticity of papier mâché aren't usually the same people that can cut glass successfully). Work out the happiest size to fit the model. Too large and it looks lost, too small is claustrophobic.

Carefully measure the depth, length and height. Two thicknesses of glass will be added to the width measurement (see the diagram). This shouldn't make much difference unless the placing of the glass case on the stand is crucial.

Add two thicknesses of glass – 6 mm ($\frac{1}{4}$ in) if it is picture glass – to the width measurement of the top and this *is* crucial, as the top pane has to rest on top of the sides. Buy glass-binding epoxy resin. (Ordinary epoxy resin will do if the other isn't available.) Clean the four edges of the glass with methylated spirit and tissue paper. You need a box roughly the same shape but smaller than the case you intend to make and one with edges at exact right angles. This is to hold the glass panes together as you wait for them to dry.

glue

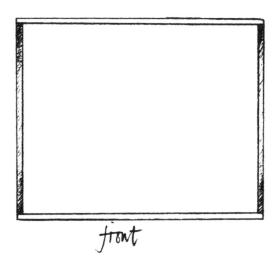

Plan showing the two side panes set inside the front and back pane

front

Then, with infinite care, glue the edge of one side pane of glass, place the front pane against it (see the diagram) and Sellotape it into position. It is easy to wipe off surplus glue from the outside with warm, soapy water on a soft cloth, but from the inside it is all but impossible, so spread the epoxy very evenly and sparingly. When this is dry according to the makers' instructions, repeat the process with the other side panel. When that is dry, the fourth and last pane is fixed, gluing both edges of the side panes at the same time.

When ready the top is carefully dropped on to the four prepared edges.

There is tremendous satisfaction in doing this carefully and unhurriedly. Go at it impatiently and you will end up furious and distraught, I promise you.

With a fine file, round off the eight sharp corner edges (ie top and sides). A 6 mm ($\frac{1}{4}$ in)-square beading should be glued and pinned around the base of the case, flush to the glass to stop it from slipping about.

Clean inside and out with methylated spirit and tissue (not window polish: the powder will get into gaps in the glue and dry white).

If you have done all that you have quite likely made a family heirloom. Well done, well done indeed.

Index